Just Plain Sadiddiness

Just Plain Sadiddiness

A Poetic Journey

Regina Y. Cooper

Just Plain Sadiddiness
© 2016 by Regina Y. Cooper

All rights reserved. No part of this book may be reproduced, stored in a retrieval system, or transmitted in any form or by any means, electronic, mechanical, photocopy, recording, scanning, or other, except for the inclusion of brief quotations in a review, without the prior written permission in writing from the author or publisher

1ST Printing October 2016

This is a work of fiction. Names, characters, businesses, places, events and incidents are either the products of the author's imagination or used in a fictitious manner. Any resemblance to actual persons, living or dead, or actual events is purely coincidental.

Published in Milwaukee, Wisconsin

Next Bestseller Publications

Cover Photo - Shutterstock Images
Cover Design by Vishal Mahagan

ISBN-10:   0-9787215-3-5
ISBN-13:   978-0-9787215-3-4

Printed in the USA

DEDICATION

To GOD, who is always amazing in HIS love and in HIS teachings and WHO is and WHO will forever be the head of my life,

To Dontre Hamilton and Sandra Bland and all of our black brothers and sisters who have and are continuing to lose their lives to senseless violence. Your lives, your existence – they matter,

To the humble sisters in this world. You are loving, protective and supportive. You build up rather than tear down the next sister. You look out and over your shoulder for her. You understand that when one sister falls, we all go down. I want to say, Thank You. You are to be commended in so many ways, yet you rarely ever are,

To those that remain in the struggle and strive each and every day, in spite of the unfair obstacles placed before them, to make the world a better place.

Charles "Chucky" Thomas

I miss you, cuz

My Promise

I promise to never become the type of writer that writes with fear in my words. I promise to always write with the honesty, boldness, rawness, hurt, humor and ultimately humanness that any real person can feel.

A Moment in Prayer

Heavenly Father, with the humblest of heart, I want to THANK YOU for assisting me in the writing of this book. Please allow it to take root where necessary and to be utilized as a tool downloaded by YOU and designed to do YOUR WILL.

I fall each night to my blackened knees in prayer to YOU. I pray that YOU watch over our sadiddy hearts and that YOU forgive us for our sometimes sadiddy ways.

Amen.

That Sadiddy Side of Us

First of all, sister, let me say that I care about us. I do. Why else would I put so much time and effort into writing this? I have a love for us that is so deep. I love how we can be so caring, so strong, and so brave when we choose to be, even during those times we truly don't want to be. We carry a phenomenal strength. It's true. But in spite of all the love and admiration that I have for us, there's this other part of us that I truly can't stand. *It's that sadiddy side of us.* That stuck-up, arrogant and highfalutin' part of us, that oftentimes tells us that we have to stand on the backs and existences of other sisters to make ourselves feel important. That we have to "talk them down" given any opportunity to do so. Come on sister, you know what I'm talking about. Let's talk about *Sadiddy*. The *she* who has gotten beneath our beautiful brown skin and has invaded our sacred spirit to the point that, well, we probably couldn't ask her to leave now, even if we really wanted her to. Deep down, we know she's there. We can feel her. But instead of fighting her like any real queen would, we have allowed her to reign. As a result, she has taken over our ability to have real, long-standing, healthy and positive connections with other sisters. And also as a result, we have allowed Sadiddy to convince us that as sisters, we are competitors. On some level, even enemies. It's a sad but truthful thing, isn't it?

I'm writing to warn you, sister, that this Sadiddy, she is a hateful thing who has to be watched. That we have to keep the most watchful eye on this trifling woman, who sets about the business of conniving her way into our spiritual doors. And once inside and having gained access to who we are and what we are capable of doing, she begins to unleash the true ugliness in us all.

Sister, as always, it is *never* my intention to further oppress or depress us in this world. The weight of the things that we are required to carry, have long since become more than we should have ever had to bear. I simply want to educate and inspire us to search more deeply within ourselves and within those findings to uproot the courage to make the necessary adjustments that will improve us as a whole.

So I write this poetic journey as an act of love for you. But please know that this is being written to myself as well. As a reminder. Because, sadiddiness, well it once reigned over me, too.

Regina

SADIDDY
(Sa/did/e)

Sadiddy is selfish; she is conceited; she is better than others; she is uptight in a stuck-up way; she is superior in her own eyes; she is above others, she is more than, pedestal perfect; she is a self-defined bitch; she is egotistical, cocky, arrogant, loudmouthed, snooty and vain; she is highfalutin, haughty, melodramatic, superficial, aloof, cavalier, domineering, overdone and pompous

She oftentimes carries the highest level of regard for herself, while doing the most amount of damage to others.

Just Plain Sadiddiness

"THAT THANG"

she was said,
to be more than any woman or man could stand
tossing her hips, all night she danced
swaying to the music of the soulful playing band

once an actress,
and a singer of song
who had a season in life
when everything went wrong,
she knew very well how to dance, she could
but was told by many that she was no good
she would audition and wait for the call
her phone never rang, nothing happened
nothing at all

so each night
she returned to drinking
and the local bar,
to be with husbands and men
who made her feel like a superstar

so lost in the world,
without a direction she would roam
following any man, just any husband home
the fact that this man
may or may not have had a wife
was never her issue, her consideration
her plight

Just Plain Sadiddiness

accused by so many wives
that she had a heart of stone,
she would remind these women
it was their husband's job to remember they had
a wife at home

and time moved forward
and never stood still
so many wives,
who just simply wanted to kill
"that thang"

who lived in the brownstone up the street
who called and tempted their husbands to meet,
her in the local motel,
the arena of secrets, the playground
the shhhh no tell

where they would lock themselves away
out of danger,
and pass a kind of sickness of love
between "that thang" and a stranger

and then there came a time
and pregnant she did land
carrying the child of man
who had never taken her hand

carrying within her a seed
without a present father,

Just Plain Sadiddiness

she now stayed at home
no longer bothered,
the local husbands

"that thang" cried all night
she no longer sang sweet songs
about affairs and infidelity that she had sewn
she humbly carried this child within her,
all alone

and anger and bitterness
became her friend
saying that she would never again,
mess with another woman's possession
she spent her time confessin'

she would be a good mother to this child inside her
that she would clean up her act
take pride in,
loving her baby girl
whom she would school and teach
everything about the world

but just as life seems to go, they say
the raising of her child didn't go that way
she pushed and pushed
until she thought that she would die,
her baby girl came out
just staring at her
and never seemed to cry

Just Plain Sadiddiness

when she went to hug her
the small child just seemed to mug her
with a look that said,
"put me back in my bed!"

and return her to bed "that thang" did
for her child was like no other kid
so she named the little girl, Sadiddy
the name itself was just something unique,
really

she had a knowing in her eyes
that said to her mother I know your lies
and all that you have done,
I give promise to you
that as your daughter,
I will be your saddest song

so cry former songbird!
Sadiddy would always say
cry as loud as you can!
the thought that it was you that birthed me,
well it's a reality that I simply can't stand

And as she took Sadiddy home,
the child grew
and there was nothing evil,
that this child wouldn't do

Just Plain Sadiddiness

she would curse her mother out
and lock her outside of the house
refuse to let her in,
she would call her mother a lying heffa,
who was just full of sin

she would bash her poor mother in the head
telling her to "get away from me I said!"

and there could be shouts
and fights heard coming from the house
there would be blood-shed and tears
with every bout,

days and nights that the police would be called
days and nights when they would be hauled
one by one out the house,
bloody fists
and torn blouse

then on her 18th birthday
Sadiddy told her mother, did say
you will suffer the most this day

you cry like never, never before
as I quiet things in this house
and finally exit that door

Just Plain Sadiddiness

and that 18th birthday came to be
and Sadiddy,
kept every promise, you see

Just Plain Sadiddiness

THE BIRTH OF SADIDDY

It's been said,

that even as a baby
Sadiddy was conceited
and never wanted to be touched,
that she kicked her small feet
and shook her soft fists
whenever she was simply told to hush

she hated the woman who birthed her

Sadiddy came into the world
feeling that her mother
should have been another
than the poor excuse for a woman that she was

her mother had little money and dirty feet
who spent her time kickin' the sheets
with the local no-good men,
Sadiddy watched her trifling mother
and vowed to become more of woman
than she had ever been

as she took her first breath
Sadiddy's no good father jumped ship,
he left

so she alone

Just Plain Sadiddiness

listened each night to the sad song
of lyrical cries that her mother shouted,
but deep inside Sadiddy with pride
kept it to herself, but doubted

that any man could love "that thang"
called her mother
an unvirtuous woman,
who had parted her vines for so many others

as soon as she began to walk
Sadiddy placed her nose up into the air
and walked around, over, above her mother
like a vain thing that just didn't care

whenever her mother spoke
Sadiddy spoke louder,
she gleamed and grinned,
at her mother's thirsty men
who now crowded around her

Sadiddy when she was alone
practiced on how to toss her hips
she taught herself to make promises
with her own sweet and youthful lips

this was something
that not even her worldly mother could do
she had outgrown her mother and deep down
well, her mother knew this, too

Just Plain Sadiddiness

so began the feud

of a Sadiddy woman and her mother
two beautiful black women under one roof
who simply couldn't stand one another

at first there were just words
then words came to blows
what happened on that Saturday night?
well to this day no one truthfully knows

but it has been said,
that on that 18th birthday
Sadiddy relieved herself of a hated burden
and took a solid metal rod
like one for hanging a curtain

and with spit-fire in her eyes
and sheer anger in her spirit
cranked up the radio
so the neighbors wouldn't hear it

blood left
blood splattered
the sound of her mother's voice, crying out
well none of that seemed to matter

down she went with that rod

Just Plain Sadiddiness

over and over again
till black was all that she could see
as her mother took her final breath in this world
Sadiddy relished in her first real taste of,
free

then Sadiddy heard that which
was sweet silence in the house
"that thang's" voice now forever quiet
it made her sing and dance about

she packed her things in a color of blood case
folded and stuffed at a steady pace

she grinned and snickered
and laughed with a wave of her hand
she was a dead-hearted daughter
who had never been her mother's fan

she opened her mother's jewelry box
and removed one ruby, one pearl
she then placed her bold fists on either hip
ready to take on her own sadiddy world

Just Plain Sadiddiness

and out into the world cold-hearted Sadiddy went…

Just Plain Sadiddiness

GIRL, SADIDDY THINKS SHE'S ALL THAT!

across the street and on the porch
the community women sat,
angry and frustrated
saying, "Girl, Sadiddy thinks she's all that!"

you see,
Sadiddy had been going with their husbands
leaving the women alone,
taking from their marriages
their kids
their home

just the other morning one of the women said
she had found one Sadiddy's earrings,
right there in her bed,
and that over to Sadiddy's front door
she was led

where she boldly told Sadiddy
she was gonna go upside her head,
told the trifling woman
that she had a house to keep clean
and most of all children to keep fed

she then saw Sadiddy again just the other day
and there her trifling self sat,
caressing her big thighs and butt

Just Plain Sadiddiness

thinking she was all that

"she got one more time
one more time", the woman said
for me to find anything of her's
in me and my husband's bed!"

then just the other night
while feeling as frustrated
and angry as she might,
she began to write
her husband some letters,

not for him but to make *herself* feel better

about all what he and Sadiddy had done
she told him about himself, you see
his lying around, his doggish ways
and how she spent her nights and days
just trying to be his good wife
trying to build them a good life

about all things,
all the things that he promised
how he had let trifling Sadiddy
come into their life, to rob them

of all they once had that was sweet and good,
that was now broken, along with her trust
because he just had to have her,

Just Plain Sadiddiness

how it was truly just lust

that took him far and away from their bed
what happened to them,
where did she and their children go, she said
how did they all get so far outside of his head?

now his once loving meals, she said
are now all cooked and filled with dread
his pies not sweet,
his cake sliced, not neat
what she puts in them now,
GOD only knows what he truly eats!

she once packed his lunches
with such happiness,
she was so sweet

but now that he had done her this way
who's really to say,
that one of these sad and sorrow-filled days
she won't cook something that would take him
forever away?

she then looked at the other women,
and rolled her eyes, saying
"maybe *it is* up to me,
to remind him of just what a husband is supposed
to be!"

Just Plain Sadiddiness

Letter #1

Dearest Heart,

As you lie here beside me, I want to tell you that I am so sick of you and your lying and cheating ways. So sick and tired of you staring me straight in the eyes and lying to me. So sick of your dishonesty about who you are and what you have to offer to me, your wife. You asked to marry me and I said yes, believing that the love gods had finally decided to show me some mercy and sent you, a good man, my way. You had me floating on the damn air. I was happy, truly happy probably for the first time in my life. That is, until that almost predictable day when you decided to… step out on me. I love you, but just like the big dog you can sometimes be, you will sniff and eat anything. Just like the dog you are, you forget all about that ring on your hand. All that it means. You forget all about the fact that you stood in God's church and before God and HIS people, my people, *your* people and swore that you loved me. You looked me deeply in the eyes, held my hand and lit candles that symbolized the fire of the love we had for each other. A candle with flames that eventually united us and forever burned us together as one. You told me and everyone you knew that yes, you loved me. That there was no other woman you wanted as your wife and I believed you,

Just Plain Sadiddiness

Dear Heart, and because of that belief, I became your wife.

Just Plain Sadiddiness

Letter #2

Dearest Husband,

As I lie here next to you, I am reminded of the fact that you purchased a home for us to share our lives together. You held my hands as we brought our children into the world. You were present when we brought our children home from the hospital. You gazed upon me and our children with a light in your eyes. A light that only a husband and father carried. And, I was secure in that light. Yes I was. I was at peace with the fact that you loved me. Otherwise, why would you have gone through all of this with me? Why would you have gone through the trouble of marrying me? Having children with me? I was not worried because I believed that ring on your hand meant something to you just as the one on my hand meant something to me. And because of this belief, it was so easy for me to kiss you on the lips that night and say, "Yes, honey, enjoy yourself out tonight with your friends. Enjoy yourself, because you are a loving, committed husband and good man to me." Just so you know, I rocked our little one to sleep when you left. She was so sweet when I kissed her cheek and laid her softly in her bed. I remember humming the last part of her lullaby and closing the door to her room. I continued to hum as I grabbed towels from the linen closet. I climbed into a warm bath. A much, so needed bath after a day of taking care of both you and our children. I slid down into the warm water and my thoughts returned to you once again, my wonderful and faithful husband. I closed my eyes and thought of our lovemaking the night before. How strong you were and how safe you made me feel, husband. I was so content with our children, our home and our life. It was around this same time when I was nestled so deeply into that water and dreaming of you, that you found a seat at the bar. One of your friends, who never believed in marriage and commitment but whom you felt the need to remain close friends with, made the comment, "Man, there sure are some nice looking women up in here, tonight?" Now until then, you had been staring down into your drink. Your mind filled with home, me and our children. Your thoughts returned to our lovemaking the other night just after the littlest one had fallen asleep. The smell of my body afterwards. The way you loved the smell of my hair and neck as we snuggled together. Your thoughts were there, until that comment and you looked up from your drink to the woman staring at you from across the bar. That woman's name was Sadiddy. Now, you claimed that you were wearing your wedding ring in clear view for the entire world to see. But that this made no difference to this woman, as she still carried lust for you in her eyes. Husband, love of my life, it never mattered to me whether or not *she* saw your wedding ring. It never mattered to me whether or not *the entire world* knew you were married. What mattered to me, the only thing that *ever mattered to me*, dear one, was that *you knew*. It was never her responsibility to remember, but yours. Now I know for a fact that I married an intelligent man. We completed college together. Started our careers together. How did you suddenly become a fool? You would have to be a fool. Why would you expect a woman like Sadiddy to have morals? Why would you expect her to have values about marriage and commitment? That, my dear husband, defeats the whole benefits of being someone like her. So the reality is that when you chose to forget, so did she. Trust and believe me when I say that it goes along with the whole loose woman's manual and playbook. And so you stared deeper than you should have, longer than any married husband or father should have. And, she came around the bar and you forgot. About me. About us. About our home. Our children. Our commitment. Our marriage. Our life. It all got lost. You forgot, as this trifling, no good woman reminded you not to forget the days when you were single and we, your family, did not exist.

Letter #3

Dearest Husband,

Love of my life, I lie here alone tonight because it is Saturday and Sadiddy has called for you. I have to ask you, where does everything that is supposed to be important to you go when you are with her? Do I just completely disappear in your mind? Our wedding vows and license just go up in flames? The children we share returned to my womb? Where does everything that are supposed to love, honor and respect go? How do you give this sad woman the power to make our entire life disappear? The fact that she knows that you are married and that she didn't care, means nothing to you. The fact that this should signal to you that she is not a good woman, didn't register. It doesn't register because things are happening inside of you. Now as your wife, I can warm you. And after so many years of marriage the flame has possibly died down to a small, but still intriguing fire. But for some reason, Sadiddy, she lights you completely ablaze. Your brain stops working when you are with her. Your rationalization and good common sense get dialed down. Your commitment to me gets disconnected like the unpaid heat bill. All you feel and recognize at that time is the uncontrollable throbbing in your pants. A throbbing that is pulling you deeper in and further away. A wave of lust enters your body and you ride it. You ride it all the way home with this woman. A home that carries no love for you, only the scent and residue of previous one night stands and brief exchanges. You enter Sadiddy's home and her bedroom. You crawl beneath her sheets. Not the sheets that I, your wife, have personally washed, ironed and folded for you. You crawl beneath, cold, unclean and contaminated sheets. Because this woman is foul and her sheets smell foul. But you excuse all of this because of the throbbing, that endless throbbing that has you going crazy. And so you allow her to put her mouth on you, my husband. You allow her to touch you, my husband. You share kisses with her. Kisses that ultimately belong to me. You give my kisses away to this trifling witch who you have allowed to put a spell on you. You enter her and our entire world changes. You give yourself to her and I can never really have you back. Not fully as my husband. You destroy all of that. The fact that my thighs and only my thighs have touched you since the marriage, has been damaged. Things are damaged beyond repair and you fail to recognize this because the throbbing is climbing and you just need it to end so that you can think again. So that you can recognize me, your children, your home and your marriage again. And so you go forward with this insane act, and the two of you

Just Plain Sadiddiness

pass feelings between each other. And this feeling is not love, because she doesn't love you and you certainly don't love her. So if it is not love that is being passed, exactly what is it?

Just Plain Sadiddiness

Letter #4

Dearest Cheater,

As I lie here beside you, I realize that you didn't care anything about me, did you? In the course of one brief encounter, this woman changed your name. You were no longer husband, love of my life, but now "cheater." She stole your honor and respect in just that short period of time. The sanctity of our marriage was tarnished and could never really be wiped clean again. She pleased herself with you and the throbbing stopped. You climbed from beneath her sheets and for a moment you felt something. Was it dirty? Grimy? Guilty? What was it? You swore to yourself and to me that you were never built for this type of dirt. If in that brief moment of time you felt cheapened, soiled, disgusted, repugnant, shameless, objectionable, odious, detestable, hideous and revolting, then you should have, because you were. You left her, Sadiddy, without a kiss because the throbbing had ceased and you could think again. You showered so that I wouldn't know. You climbed into our bed and inside of me because you thought I didn't know. Your mouth searched for the lips that you knew held and would respond with love for you. Your body searched between my thighs for the opening to me that was available to you, because you also knew that in that place in that soft place there would be love waiting for you. That soft place was home. You didn't have to seek it. It was already there. You awoke and sat across from me at the breakfast table, a familiar loving face. Only to find what? That somewhere inside of you, we were now strangers. And no matter how hard you tried, you just couldn't seem to get Sadiddy's dirt off of you. And no matter how much you desired to, you could never get back what you left inside of her. The sad thing being, it was the same thing you left inside of me to make our beautiful brown babies. And, former love of my life, little did you know that, Sadiddy, was a friend of a friend of mine. And because she was a "trifling, unhappy witch" and because sadiddy women like this have no true code of honor or need for any valor or respect, she wanted to make sure that it got back to me. And back to me it did. One night when I was with my girls playing spades and doing "our thang" and we had won the last book. We had just ran us a "Boston" and your "tricks-are-for-kids" witch blurted out the realities of *our* life to me. She blurted out the dishonesty of *my husband*. You. She purposely did this in front of our children. And like the woman, the true woman that you married, I, with calm and purposeful execution, covered our babies ears and took our beautiful innocent children home. I tucked our babies into the safety and comfort of the home we bought together. I kissed each one of them on the cheek and went down to the kitchen that you had gotten remodeled for me. I opened the stainless steel drawer and withdrew from it my justice. Long, sharp and serrated. I climbed the stairs and entered our bedroom. I stood over you, cheater. I stood over you and looked down upon you. You looked so peaceful. So far away. I blinked through mascara smeared eyes, trying to hold back the flood of tears that seemed to weigh so heavily upon me. Tears that truly were my body's rain. I raised my justice above your sleeping body and drew it back as far as I could. You seemed to lie in the perfect position. On your back, arms stretched wide open. As if you both expected as well as desired death.

Just Plain Sadiddiness

Letter #5

Dear Separation,

And wouldn't you know it, just as I was about to end my suffering that night, one of our babies appeared in the hallway outside our room. She looked so beautiful standing there in her pink pajamas and rubbing her eyes. Asking for her daddy. Asking for you, separation. She crawled into the bed next to you and for some reason still unknown to me, she draped her body directly across yours as you slept. As if to protect you. Saving you somehow, from me? As I placed a blanket over the two of you, I seemed to return to myself once again. I left the bedroom and found myself back at the stainless steel drawer, placing what I had taken from it back inside. I then grabbed the car keys from the counter and returned to where Sadiddy was. I want you to know what when I found her she was with another woman's husband. Please don't fool yourself into believing that you meant anything to her. You didn't. You were just another bump in the road. Another fool on Sadiddy's hit list. I realized that she was never going to stop damaging other women. But I just had to lay hands on her. And she fought hard, I want you to know that, because that was just the kind of woman that she was. A woman who would fight you, even though she knows that she is in the wrong. I needed to beat out on her all of the pain and sadness that she had brought into my life. That you, Separation, had opened the door for her to do. And, as I pushed my foot down on *her face*, I could only see *your face*. You, sleeping so soundly next to our baby girl. Not knowing that I, your wife, was somewhere in the world being forced to act like a thug and standing on top of the end of our marriage. And all while that we battled through our divorce proceedings and all the emotional war that it rained over us and over our sweet babies, you never once said that you were sorry and meant it. Your apologies only seemed to come from a place that was sorry that you got caught. How dare you fail to recognize the damage that this has done to me as a woman and wife! How dare you fail to recognize what this will do to our children! You cheated me out of our connection and trust. You cheated our children out of really knowing what love, commitment and marriage between a man and a woman should really be like. We were all cheated because you weren't man enough to control and take power over your own body. Your body needed a ten minute exchange with someone else. Well, you got it, and so did I. I found out not too much later from the nurse at the clinic who spoke and looked upon me as if I was a trick in the street tossing myself to every Tom, Dick and husband. And not the woman who I really was. The faithful wife to you. Who had never even had the remotest thought to step out on you because I was in love with loving you. Just that simple. I was so in love with loving you that I somehow forgot to love myself. I used to run three miles a day just to stay healthy for you and our children. I ate right. Stayed fit. Everything tight and right for you. Just trying to be and stay that trophy piece that you and your friends required me to be. The pressure to be a "dime" and to stay a dime was never-ending. Because any real woman knows, she must fully realize, that she has to get both your approval as well as your boy's approval to be cuffed. Right? I did everything you asked, became everything you needed and provided everything you wanted and what did I get in return? A liar. A cheater. A separation and a low-life. You must understand, hurting someone is not built into my nature. Not at all a part of my DNA. But when you hurt me, you somehow add this to my repertoire. You pull me completely out of my character. And I start to do things that go against everything that I believed in or ever saw myself doing. But to have ended your life, would have ended mine. And it would took me away from my babies. So I allow you to live. But I want you to realize and truly understand that the fact that you and Sadiddy are still living is a gift like no other. You should have died that night and I should be sitting on death row. But the God in me is strong. Stronger than I ever imagined. But because of you half father, half husband and half man. Because of you and your half woman, Sadiddy, I now take twenty-seven pills a day just so our children can have a whole mother. Former husband, don't you realize that you had the opportunity to give me two types of love? The one that could make me completely float on air and the other one that could completely shatter my existence. You chose the latter. It's a pain that is probably so unknown to you. It is a pain that is indescribable. And the betrayal? It's probably something that you will never truly understand. It is a hateful crime.

Just Plain Sadiddiness

MATRIMONIAL MURDER AND ALL YOUR OTHER HATEFUL CRIMES

you have committed a horrendous crime
you've basically been found out,
and have been found guilty
on all the devious counts

but it is now, dear heart
that your sentence and pain
truly starts

so once former love of my life,
who allowed a whore to steal our life,
you no longer have to sneak around
worrying about being seen or found,

but this is what comes next for you
you must forget all about me and your children,
you do

and go out into the world brand new

to see if your sweet Sadiddy
will *even* have you

Just Plain Sadiddiness

TRIANGLE

*two angles, three sides
back and forth between his wife and Sadiddy
he glides,
never realizing that last night they both cried
words of love were spoken,
real honesty denied*

*I love you,
he testified,*

*altering, mind twisting, changing their insides
taking them on a merciless ride
to a place where they can't hide
not even from themselves,
used like rag dolls, toys
placed back on silly shelves*

*triangle
two angles, three sides,
back and forth between two women
he glides
not knowing that as he spins his lies
something inside each of them dies
that they collide
and somehow become one*

*The same one woman
the same hurt*

the same pain
the same distrust

it's at this point that he must
stop, drop and roll
give into his dishonesty
save at least one sister's soul

redeem himself
before he hits the grave
realizing that he took far more
than he ever gave.

triangle
two angles, three sides,
back and forth between
two sisters he glides

where will this brother be
once all the sisters have been tried?

Just Plain Sadiddiness

YOU GOT TO BE SOME KIND OF FOOL, TO THINK THAT SADIDDY EVER REALLY WANTED YOU!

having now left his wife
for a sadiddy-filled kind of life
he never thought for a moment that day
that his sweet Sadiddy
wouldn't allow him to stay

and when he showed up at Sadiddy's door
thinking what they had was more
believing Sadiddy would care that he was sad,
he found her empty and cold
that he had simply been a bump in her road

telling him that the sex
was all that night was for
that she was done with him, they were done
there was no further need
for him to knock on her door
because that night
he had simply fulfilled a need
that there was no point for him to plead

and tried as he did
to make things light,
Sadiddy gave him the coldest stare
closed the door,
and turned out her light

Just Plain Sadiddiness

and as picked up his bags
all that he had,
he was left a broken man
a used man
a husband so sad

and as he walked down the street that day
the last words of his former wife
came to his mind in that way

she had told him,
that it was his time to be schooled,
"cause you got to be some kind of fool,
to think that Sadiddy *ever* really wanted you!"

Just Plain Sadiddiness

and in spite of all the damage that she had done
in spite of the pain that she caused,
Sadiddy never paused, not once

Sadiddy was pompous and arrogant
in all of her conceited glory

but it is important
so important,
that you know her *entire* story

Just Plain Sadiddiness

THE SADIDDY STRUT

She walks the street
with her nose turned to the sky,
gives you the coldest stare as she walks by
she is cold, angry, dead inside
your best bet is just to step aside
she is black and blue
ain't got time for you
don't let her smooth exterior fool you
she'll be the first to school you
on her ability to condescend
'cause she's a sadiddy, black thing

Sadiddy,

right down to her sadiddy black skin

Just Plain Sadiddiness

GIRL, GONE SOMEWHERE WIT YO SADIDDY SELF!

a sadiddy thing was what she had been called
by both men and women alike
big was how she talked
an arrogant woman,
who stood hard on and occupied all the ground she walked

and spoke from the sweetest of lips
with an uppity appeal,
a condescending attitude
how and whenever she would feel

there were those who wanted to scratch her
those who wanted to match her
but she only sashayed past them
with a pompous smirk on her lips,
pulling her dress around her a little tighter
saying," Look here at these big, pretty hips!"

the word bitch didn't move her
the word bitch didn't prove her
she had no fear of a five-letter word,
she was a stuck-up, steel-hearted sister
with a look in her eyes that shouted,
"I don't care what the hell you've heard!"

Just Plain Sadiddiness

she never stopped to say hello
never stopped to even speak,
she was fine enough with a switch in her walk
that made all the husbands weak
because you see,
she was a sadiddy witch with an astounding itch
to let all the world know,
she's was a black rebel, an ebon queen
no otha sister was even close to her level

she would threaten sisters
to put a hush on their words
whatever they had to say,
she wasn't one to take things lightly
in other words, this mean, snooty heffa didn't play

because she had been born sadiddy
she had never been hurt, defeated,
abused or mistreated
born into the world with a ready-made
heart of black stone

but the men?
in spite of this,
they simply couldn't leave sweet Sadiddy alone

Just Plain Sadiddiness

I CAN'T STANDS ME NO SADIDDY WOMAN!

and alone she never was
the reason,
the why,
the because

she had a beauty that brought a desire
and a moisture to men's lips
a wetness that begged for just small sips,
of her

she would make orders in bed
do this, do that
now, I said!

and the men loved it
they didn't mind it, not even one single drop
even when she would cut them
at the brink of their horizon
by simply telling them to "stop"

and like mischievous, mannish bees
the men would often come in droves
freeing up their always faithful wives
in pursuit of anytime available easy street hoes

they wanted just a taste of her sweet honey,

Just Plain Sadiddiness

just a moment of sweet Sadiddy's time

and her time?

it was never cheap
she was a smart woman, who handled her business
so all the money she made was hers to keep

Sadiddy had,
men paying her car note
men paying her bills
keeping company with them and keeping it good
was Sadiddy's only part of the deal

and after a while the money she made
was enough for what she planned to do
so she sought out the most beautiful
sisters in the neighborhood
became an entrepreneur and started her own crew

of beautiful, perfectly shaped, bold sisters
who knew what to do and could
Sadiddy had a way of just looking at a woman
and knowing, instinctively, if she were any good

deep down Sadiddy hated these other women
even the ones she didn't know
she saw them as the enemy, the competition
and if Sadiddy had ever failed to mention
these women were useless females,

Just Plain Sadiddiness

empty-headed bores
simpletons she might even say
who were just jealous of the beauty that she wore

she would roll her eyes at women
even talk about them behind their back
she would conceitedly recognize her own perfection
but purposely point out all that they lacked

she made it clear to these women
that they were never to be friends
Sadiddy was too caught up,
too preoccupied, too focused
on all the callous, no-good men

in spite of this
Sadiddy would find herself
wondering time and time again,
asking herself, deeply questioning, just truly who were
these men?

Just Plain Sadiddiness

BEAUTIFUL DARK CREATURES

who are these men,
are they conniving, dark or mad,
are they fragile to the touch
envious in their hearts
jealous of what we sisters have?

who are these men,
who slip through our loving fingers
who leave in the blink of an eye,
who sometimes don't remain in the picture long
enough to really give our love a try

to be honored and revered as no less
to be seen by them as the best
a sister can get no rest
as she fails their always unpassable test

who are these men,
beneath their concealing masks
beneath their fake smiles
beneath their misleading eyes
who are these dark creatures who unfold
unforgivable lies?

who are these men,
men that we try to hold onto so tight
reaching for them through the darkness
and into the night,

Just Plain Sadiddiness

we are blinded by the hope of their love
their love sometimes manipulating our sight

who are these men,
put into place by life
supposedly to defend us,
who spend their days and focus their ways
on simply trying to end us

these men who are no longer knights, but *our nights*
dark times with them behind us and ahead
always doubtful of where they are taking us
just where in fact we are being led

down roads and places we never wanted to be
locked outside of their love with no key
we stand around the map of the world
just praying at some point for their love to unfurl

so with the humblest of heart,
we simply ask again
can anyone tell us,
who *exactly* are these men?

Just Plain Sadiddiness

SWEET SADIDDY'S TIME

and these men?
they paid well for her world of sadiddiness
and with so many women now working for her
Sadiddy could do less and less

"I can't stands me no sadiddy woman!"
she would often hear the men say,
as they gathered up their work clothes with gratitude
and vulnerably counted out all that week's pay

"I got's me a good wife at home, Sadiddy!
don't need to come here no more!"
she would often hear the men say
while she pulled out her appointment book
and all the while looked,
for an open day,
for this so-called committed black man
to find his husband recess
she knew he would be back to play

they often would leave her with a look of guilt
swearing up and down that they were good men,
never built
for this type of dirt

Sadiddy often thought if their wives only knew
how hurt,

Just Plain Sadiddiness

they would be
to know their bodies weren't enough to really set
their men free

each day,
Sadiddy watched from her shaded window
that overlooked the busiest and noisiest train track
she patiently perched and waited
as each new sunrise brought the unfaithful men
back

Just Plain Sadiddiness

SADIDDY SUNRISES

because Sadiddy knew

that with each new sunrise
each brand new day,
a man only really thought of one thing
the whens, hows and wheres of his next lay

she often laughed, a narcissistic laugh
at the wives who thought they had faithful men,
didn't they know that sunrises
awoke liars and cheaters
and brought in from the horizon unforgiveable,
unspeakable sin?

and because of this,

Sadiddy only thought of one thing
how to get more husbands, more men to come
how to get into their wallets and pockets
take more money from

their children, their wives, their lives

to Sadiddy these people were faceless
didn't mean a thing,
she thought of how she would dethrone
any woman in order to remain queen

Just Plain Sadiddiness

if Sadiddy could do anything well
she thought she knew how to love herself
she made a vow never
to be any man's ragdoll, silly plaything
to be removed and placed back on the shelf

Just Plain Sadiddiness

HIS THROW AWAY SHELF

it was built and designed
by his own construction
was it built, sister
somehow built for our eventual destruction?

as we have become his toy
to be picked up and played with at his will,
our bodies twisted, limbs manipulated
he never even stops to ask us how we feel

for now we are new to him
we might even have that new car smell
we fascinate him, don't we?
with our pretty black selves

then he rolls us through the dirt of his life
and messes our freshly done hair
bored and done with us now
we are placed on his throw away shelf

next to the others that are there
others he promised that he cared
now who just sit and stare
brown-eyed and empty,
hollow to the core
there he goes, girl
back to the always available sister store

Just Plain Sadiddiness

to buy a whole new one to play with
a man really ever loving one woman?
well, it's all just a myth

look at our once pretty self
now all messed up beneath our hair
nose turned up in the air
all covered in his dirt,
we are like plastic to him now
no longer even real enough to hurt

there we sit, girl
brown-eyed and empty
making no attempt to even climb down
no real will left in us to try to make a sound

was it that we somehow failed to pay attention,
how did we become a part of this sad, sociopathic
collection?

do we fail to understand
that this is where we land
with our poseable self,
there we sit brown-eyed and empty
now a full member of his throw away shelf

Just Plain Sadiddiness

VAINGLORIOUS

at her own will
Sadiddy knew how to kill
to steal a man's heart,
she knew how to manipulate him, bait him
get him to part

with whatever she needed
she had no cravings for a man's love
so there was no need to feed it

so each evening
she sat alone
with the exception of her money beside her,
and thought of new ways
and made new vows
that no man would ever ride her
for free

yes, there was a woman inside of Sadiddy,
but no man would ever bring her to her knees!

the men said, "I love you Sadiddy!
she would say "I love you, too" in sweet tease,
but Sadiddy loved no one, she only loved herself
that was all that she could see
she would often look lovingly into her mirror
saying

Just Plain Sadiddiness

"Can't nobody love Sadiddy more than Sadiddy love me!"

she held herself in the highest regard
with the highest level of esteem
she was told every woman needs a good man
even when it doesn't seem

but not Sadiddy

in her own eyes she was a mold-breaker
and felt this was what
the women and men didn't get
so day after day Sadiddy sat vaingloriously alone,
and watched quietly

for the sins of the sunset

Just Plain Sadiddiness

SADIDDY SUNSETS

and the sins came,

they came in moans and groans
from husbands who should have been home
in hives, with wives
who had stove-top stuffing waiting
anticipatin'

the arrival of him

Sadiddy knew in the back of their minds
thoughts of home came and went
as what was being done to them,
sent

waves of gotta have's through their flesh
it bothered them, deep down
no matter how hard they tried
the truth was that they just couldn't seem to mesh
with their own wives in that way

how had things gotten so stale,
how had they gotten so far away?

from the whens of pleasing each other
running home at the end of the day
to find one another,

Just Plain Sadiddiness

to come together one more time under the sheets
where a husband and wife find each other
where their most intimate love is supposed to meet

but Sadiddy listened as men arrived
with an almost anger
feelings shared and manipulated
between them and an uninhibited stranger

she knew men were only faithful
while at their wives' sides
that they were good at deceiving, fooling
real good in their ability to hide
what happens at the sunsets
but Sadiddy vowed, never
never to forget

she knew that a woman
parted and divorced with much too much
for the five seconds of so-called love
they found in a so-called man's touch

she knew that a wife, a real wife
was always seeking vengeance
trapped behind the walls of a marriage
that had slowly over time become a sentence

twenty years to life
days full of stress and strife
to her that didn't sound like happiness,

Just Plain Sadiddiness

didn't resemble home
so she discovered the peacefulness of solitude
and became quite content with being alone

Just Plain Sadiddiness

WHEN LONELINESS MOVES IN

and alone she was
and doing fine, that is
until something so unexpected and so uninvited
decided to move in

the truth be told
Sadiddy sat in her condo alone
with a phone that never rang,
she often thought about that Saturday
her mother, that "thang"

the quiet stillness of her home
had begun to create a pang in her heart
that started to make her wonder
how she had gotten so far apart
from the world

then in her moment of quiet reflection
her moment of self-inspection
there came a knock at Sadiddy's door,
this intrusion irritated her as she wondered
just what in the hell they were there for

she pulled her sadiddy self up
from her unimportant couch
and allowed her feet to hit the floor,
there was an ugly scowl on her face,

Just Plain Sadiddiness

that left no trace
that happiness had ever lived there before

Sadiddy had gotten to be mean, lonely
angry, but still rich
what she found on the other side of her door,
waiting
was Loneliness that ugly, gray-haired bitch

Loneliness never waited to be invited in
just gave Sadiddy a slight grin
that sent chills through her,
she looked knowingly into Sadiddy's eyes
like a long-time friend
as if she knew her?

Loneliness placed her dirty bags
and all that she was able
upon the center of Sadiddy's much paid for,
meaningless cocktail table
she sat down hard in Sadiddy's favorite chair
and using one finger to pull back her hair,
from her face
she looked into the eyes of Sadiddy
and told her this home was now *their* place

for the first time
Sadiddy felt something in her heart
it could only be imagined that it was fear
the look in the woman eyes

Just Plain Sadiddiness

the foul smell of the woman's breath
whenever Sadiddy came near

Loneliness, with daggers in her eyes
stared at and through Sadiddy
she called her a selfish, arrogant woman

for whom she had no pity

"Get the hell out of my house!"
Sadiddy shouted and said
"or I'ma kill you!"

Loneliness only cackled and said,
"You might, Sadiddy, but instead
think about how you're going to kill that
which is already dead!"

and in spite of all Sadiddy said
in spite of how much she pled,
Loneliness only undressed herself
and climbed into Sadiddy's bed

and in sweet Sadiddy's bed
Loneliness then turned her shoulder,
Sadiddy stood there, watching her thinking this
intrusive heffa,
just couldn't be any colder

and Loneliness stayed on

Just Plain Sadiddiness

OUR FEAR OF LONELINESS

we run from her
like a cat scared in the night
'cause we just can't stand the way
that she makes us feel
not wanting to deal,
with the woman inside of us that's blue
when we have a fear of loneliness
what is a woman supposed to do?

we take to the streets and bars
just simply searching for a lover,
choosing users, abusers and low-lifes
sometimes rummaging through the gutter
looking for anything, just anything
even remotely resembling a man,
its sad how we take pride in bragging
about someone that is so less than

we take the most careful steps
not to give others the slightest hint,
that everything is not so sweet and cozy
that we are in fact paying the rent

we flash on our finger a glass wedding ring
that we happily describe in every layer,
we include every detail of the lie-story
accept the part that we, ourselves, were the payer

Just Plain Sadiddiness

each night he pulls at us
as he quickly pulls back the bedding,
watching for his fool he can trust
who is dumb enough to pay for her own wedding

and each day,
that we spend with our supa-duper man of nothing
our heart and minds begin to mingle,
with thoughts of the past,
times we would laugh
when we free and single

but you know,
Loneliness knows that we fear her
she knows that we see her
sitting so comfortably in the corner of our lives
never straying far enough to truly leave our eyes

she is there to throw shade
when we cry, that's how her joy is made
that this dull pain in our heart never fades
this is how Loneliness gets her pay

it is most often our fear of loneliness
that oftentimes is owning us
and keeps us in relationships that we shouldn't be

in other words,
Loneliness *is* a gray-haired bitch

Just Plain Sadiddiness

but moreso she is simply,
our greatest fear,
our fear of being devoid
our fear of being just completely empty

Just Plain Sadiddiness

MEN IN SHADES OF GREEN, BLACK, AND BLUE

and Loneliness stayed on

she told Sadiddy of the men that were to come
with hearts that would be green, black or blue
that after rummaging through all of these men
there would be one among them to say "I love you"

that he would only ask for one return
that she open her heart in concern
and honestly love him

she then threatened to stay
in a way that was so clever
that if Sadiddy never dropped her stuck-up ways
that she, Loneliness, would stay on forever

so after sometimes and somedays
Sadiddy could think of no worse fate,
than to have Loneliness at her fragile side
as a forever hateful roommate

so Sadiddy anxiously awaited these so-called men
and one by one, year after year
they eventually came in

and what men they were

Just Plain Sadiddiness

ten, hundreds, thousands per
but none that met the perfect standards of her

all shapes, sizes and different looks
but none, not one, who took
Sadiddy's breath away
she vented to Loneliness
who only rolled her impatient eyes
and again made her promise to stay

time after time
as Sadiddy sorted through the men,
it was amazing how she found
something wrong with each one of them

he was too tall
he was too short
this one didn't laugh enough
this one laughed with an annoying snort

Sadiddy herself wanted perfection
a beautiful black man, with perfect teeth
a flawless complexion

she wanted him thick and strong
who would never accuse her of being wrong
she wanted him faithful and capable of
everything she needed,
who would allow her to look into the mirror
yet never accuse her of being conceited

Just Plain Sadiddiness

she wanted to be allowed to still see other men
a man who wouldn't bend her ability to be who
she wanted to be
Sadiddy needed just the right man
a perfectly, perfect one you see

but Loneliness remained on
she even started to unpack her things
and placed some items on Sadiddy's sad shelf,
Loneliness realized this woman would be forever lonely
for she could think of no one other than herself

each night Loneliness listened
to the painful cries of Sadiddy
a lost woman, with no ability
to see outside of her own needs
who now got down each night, kneeling
raising her brown head to the ceiling

she got angry, stumped her feet
and realized that it all was a pity
that no one in the entire world
had written a prayer just for her,
a prayer just for Sadiddy!

A PRAYER FOR A SADIDDY WOMAN

I pray for you every day, my sister
I pray for your sadiddy ways,
when you refuse to correctly love your children
and keep your bills paid

ways and attitudes
that keep you defeated and down,
when you are so lazy in mind and spirit
that no form of inspiration can be found

ways that keep you from recognizing
the beauty of your own kids,
all the hugs, sloppy kisses
and "I love you's" that stay hid

when you choose to love everything else instead,
stay all day occupied with nothing in bed
when you never pay attention
to how you are being led
further away from the importance of your babies,
while you waste time laying up with funky baby
daddy
and recycled baby daddy-maybes?

too sadiddy to even ask for help or how to
ask you about your goals,
plans for the future?

Just Plain Sadiddiness

sister, you have no clue

cause your days and mind are full
with all about what you
and your no good man will do,
you only call other sisters and family
when you, yourself are feeling blue

a selfish sister,
too conceited to try to do better
for the love of your daughter or son,
you spend the majority of your energy
just trying to keep your hair and nails done

a sadiddy one,
too selfish to settle down to one place
you are constantly moving your children
from corner to corner,
house to house,
street to street,
state to state

you are too sadiddy to look into future's eyes
refusing to recognize
your babies have tired of your reckless life

while ill-hearted men down you
hungry-for-love children crowd around you
they orbit you,
you've lost your ability to love outside of yourself

Just Plain Sadiddiness

the light for this luxury has gone blue

girl, your lights been turned off again,
again I ask you, what are you gonna do?
I pray for you and your pretend pedestal
yet every day you play in the dirt,
play with dirty men,
play dirty games
tell dirty lies
get hurt

too sadiddy to keep yourself in check
you walk around, uncovered, a wreck
reveal your flesh,
silently screaming to the world that this is the best
that you have to offer
trying to act all hard, but you couldn't be any softer

I pray for you sadiddy sister
when you won't get out of bed to search for a better life
while you sit on rotting porches
drink forty ounces
and claim you never wanted to be a wife

I pray for you, girl,
I say, "Gone witcha stuck-up self!"

but it saddens me

Just Plain Sadiddiness

breaks my heart
to find you, girl
still on life's throw-away shelf

Just Plain Sadiddiness

HOW CONCEITED SISTERS PRAY

I dance,
with voluptuous God-given swinging hips
I pray,
with less than humble lips

Sister, I tell you
I pray when things start to go bad
but not out of belief or faithfulness
but I fall to my knees, like it's a fad

I pray

then for a long time I forget
my mind so caught up in *him's, not hymns*
who cruise the street in shiny cars
with dizzying, spinning rims

this is how I pray

then I stop
till things go bad again

this is how I pray

I pray sister, I do
for both me and you, a blessin'
I pray for things to get better

Just Plain Sadiddiness

but how can they?
when I don't accept the lesson

I don't learn from it, I just repeat it
I never attempt to defeat it

this is how I pray,
nothing wrong with praying I'm told
but you see,
I'm guilty of praying only when I'm I trouble
when I need God to pay attention to me
to free me from my own self-made,
messed up bubble
that I, myself, have blown air and life into
when my problems get so deep sometimes
I just don't know what to do

this is how I pray,
It's like a dance to me
when I feel the heat, the burn
it moves me
collapsing me to my knees
I'm dancing the dance of the arrogant praying
sister, you see

look, I ain't got time for this
I don't care what you say,
as a conceited, stuck-up sister,
this is how I pray!

Just Plain Sadiddiness

YOU CAN GET THINGS DONE ALL BY YOURSELF, SADIDDY!

And pray Sadiddy did everyday
asking God for HIS grace,
that a perfect love be sent her way

the men came in shades of green
who envied everything she owned
and had worked for,
it seemed

they came in shades of black
as their hearts seemed to lack
any ability to love her for
who she truly was,
molding her to be their personal slave
insisting that it was what a woman does

then they came in shades of blue
some so bruised and broken in spirit
she didn't know what to do

there was one in particular
a lazy no good man,
who wanted to stay at home everyday
because he was stay-on-the-couch fan

this man had no ambition
no intention to fix anything in the house

Just Plain Sadiddiness

who only laid his tired, unmotivated ass
all day on Sadiddy's already paid for couch

it was all so sad
it was all such a pity,
all he ever said was
"You can get things done all by yourself,
Sadiddy!"

You get things done all by yourself, Sadiddy!
that was all she ever heard
when they made love it was empty
and nothing inside of her stirred

no longer just being black
but now feeling blue,
Sadiddy was tired of the waves of different men
and all they didn't do

this man was no help to her
not any help to her really,
each day he awoke saying,
"You can get things done all by yourself,
Sadiddy!"

his folk-kin arriving unannounced
coming to stay
most times for twenty-nine nights
and an extra day,
she eventually asked this man to leave

Just Plain Sadiddiness

to be on his way
that he could no longer
lay around her house all day

not long thereafter,
there came a familiar knock at the door
and there she stood in all her grayness,
with that awful stinky, dirty hair
Sadiddy searched the eyes of Loneliness
who only reminded her
that she truly never went anywhere

Sadiddy cried out into the darkness
that the emptiness inside her
just couldn't be tolerated another day
in full despair and with much pain
Sadiddy's tears came down like the rain

Just Plain Sadiddiness

And it was during that night that the most powerful of all voices began to speak to her

Just Plain Sadiddiness

TEARS ARE THE BODY'S RAIN

there something about our tears, sister
that's supposed to wash away our pain
like the rain beating down on us
making us like new again

but when the tears swell in our eyes
and run down the side of our smooth brown face
there can be found no trace,
for rain often falls quietly
and tears come at us like a train
a motive so out of control
when there's nothing left to gain

when we are feeling so empty inside
when our face and eyes, can't hide
from the pain in the roof of our minds
girl, why does our lives feel so much,
like it's raining all the time?

tears are the body's rain
they fall on the rooftops of our pain
then they splash and collide
with the pain in our heart
making us question when did this rain ever start?

our tears are like
our body, spirit and minds releasing a rain
while we attempt to heal, bandage ourselves

Just Plain Sadiddiness

and dodge the puddles of pain
tears are the body's rain

Just Plain Sadiddiness

SADIDDY, YOU POOR LOST WOMAN, COME ON IN HERE FROM THAT RAIN!

And this most powerful voice
spoke to Sadiddy and
HE said,

sadiddy woman,
come on in from the rain
don't you know it's you, my child
that's keeping you in so much pain?

cause earthly man can only bring into your life
the hurt you allow him to
he can't alter your beautiful
sun-kissed cocoa color
unless you allow him to

he can't change you to blue
if you know how to receive love and give love
without allowing it to steal from you

he can't make your tears
come down like the rain

oh, LORD
oh, SWEET LORD, she cried!
what is a sadiddy sister like me to do?

other than find hopeless reasons

Just Plain Sadiddiness

to ride each season into the next,
how am I supposed to give love
if it hasn't been given to me yet?

LORD, how does a sadiddy woman like me, find her way in from the rain?

And the LORD began to speak and when HE spoke HE told her of the different seasons that she would have to endure…

And because HE was the Truth and The Light, these seasons for Sadiddy came to pass...

SEASONS OF SADIDDY

her Spring came
yet offered her pretty much of the same
without her choice,
just quiet times and conversation
with This Most Powerful Voice

her Summer came
offering her a new warmth in her heart
allowing her to part with some of the arrogance
that she kept,
she began feel different, be different
to look out for her sisters, to help

getting to know them
teaching them how to become wiser and stronger,
realizing these sisters
were not her enemy, her competition
at least not any longer

Sadiddy had always used her conceit
as a means of keeping immunity,
but the LORD led her back, sent her back
right into her own community

to clean up the mess that she had created
to give reparation to the community she had
shaded

Just Plain Sadiddiness

to clean up the women
she had so poorly done and used
to assist them, help them
especially the ones she refused

she willingly became their foot stool
and allowed these women to rise upon her back
she humbled herself, bowed her head
helping each one of them to get back on track
she apologized to all the women
for all that she had robbed from their lives
asking them for their forgiveness
as she slowly began removing all the knives

that she had placed so deceptively
into the back of each and every one of them
Sadiddy began to share and laugh
with these women
actually become closer with them

and Sadiddy began to see
the women in a new light
there for her to have and love,
never there for her to slight

streams of dreams
showing her community so clean
began to flood into her sleep
she spoke out to her community, made promises
and every promise she did keep

Just Plain Sadiddiness

she saw the women there for one another
she saw the community
around her begin to improve
she was constantly bringing things they needed
wanting to know if there was more she could do

and even in spite of all the hard work
of that particular season,
her Summer had become her favorite
and this was for good reason

but the test of her seasons were still to come
she still had yet to endure her Winter and Fall
and the LORD said to her,
"Sadiddy, now these seasons are usually the hardest of all."

Just Plain Sadiddiness

GIRL, WHAT YOU DOING OUT THERE IN THAT COLD?

her Winter rolled in hard
it was a cold and uncomfortable feeling
when she looked back over her life
she understood it was a part of the healing

her Winter came in hard from the harshness
of how she had treated others
most of all her trials had come,
the LORD had said
from how she had treated her mother

then came her biggest test
it seemed to be her tribulation season,
for it was during this time the LORD
ceased to talk to her with truly no good reason

her Fall came from the people
whom she hadn't allowed herself to love
the people she had done so wrong
feeling the blues,
her heart broke like that of a sad song

and because the LORD had ceased to talk to her,
she returned to her former days
went back to her former sadiddy ways
she parted her sacred temple for strangers
and dodged and stayed clear

Just Plain Sadiddiness

of the wrong men, you know
any men who tried to change her

she flaunted her perfect breasts and butt
and dared heated men not to touch
what she had on display
but doing these things, being in these places
it no longer felt okay

she needed someone to truly love her in their heart
no longer wanting to be seen as just a piece,
a man who would take ownership,
purchase her by marriage
not just lease,
her for the night
sleeping with all these different men
in poor Sadiddy's heart just no longer felt right

these men loved the way she looked
loved the way she smelled
but none really cared for her
or cared how she truly felt

so that night
after much stress and strife,
the LORD began to speak

HE began to tell her how
HE needed to see where her faith was now
HE promised her that

Just Plain Sadiddiness

HE would always be there for the rest,
that she had turned away from her former life,
that she had passed HIS biggest test!

that if she could do as she was told
there would be blessings for her, blessings
better than gold

that she must vow to sleep with not another man
who wouldn't bring her closer to HIM
or ask her for her hand

and Sadiddy agreed,
for it was HIM and not herself
that she wanted to please

and this new vow wasn't easy at all
for when a woman has had a man inside her
something deep just seems to call,
out for more of it
that sweet, warm feeling
that they have to fight to resist

and so,
Sadiddy's love came down hard
like large black boulders between her hips
but no matter how hard that feeling came
no matter how it shook her
no matter how she sweated in desire
no matter how many times it took her

Just Plain Sadiddiness

Sadiddy kept her promise
she held her virtue on the shelf
no matter what the temptation
Sadiddy stayed strong and held herself

she kept her black vines crossed

and she carried this vow for many, many long years…

Just Plain Sadiddiness

DIDN'T YO MAMA EVER TELL YOU, GIRL, TO KEEP YOUR GOODIES IN THE BAG?

didn't you mama ever tell you, girl
to keep your goodies in the bag
ain't no man gonna ever marry
someone that everyone else has had

so make him wait on it
like he's never waited on nothing before
for a locomotive that may or may not be coming
maybe two o'clock, three o'clock or maybe four?

don't you give him nothing before that ring,
no matter how much you date
sister put him on your possibility shelf
next to the others,
make him wait

take the time to study him
get to know his kin folks
to the point that you can call his mother "ma'am"
watch how he treats the one's he supposed to love
put together your *own* exam

but make him wait
like a pot that's waiting to boil,
let him simmer and then stir him a few times
then throw in a little blessing oil

Just Plain Sadiddiness

but keep your goodies in a bag
hold onto them for dear life
stop running around
lying to yourself and others
saying you never want to be a wife

because it takes time for him to find his rib
but believe me when he does,
he will give you all the love that you desire
he will give you all the things your heart will admire

but keep your goodies in the bag
and make him wait
if he leaves you for it,
simply understand that he was never a part of your fate

but while you are waiting and
wondering what to do
take the time to study, girl
take the time to study, you

Just Plain Sadiddiness

SOMETIMES WAITING CAN FEEL LIKE DYING

she is dying,
she is

without him
without his presence
without him near
love can be handed to her in its lowest form,
but he can still convince her that it's real

she is dying

although she still walks and talks among the living
she is slowly dying with her love imprisoned inside her
no place for the giving

she is dying

so drowned in crying
so drowned in denying
that she needs be loved

she stays trapped inside her own sadiddy being
too many attempts at love,
perspiring, bleeding
upon and within her own black soul
sometimes a woman's heart

Just Plain Sadiddiness

can stop believing for awhile
sometimes, it can just go so cold.

sometimes waiting can feel like dying

Just Plain Sadiddiness

A MAN OF GOLD

It's been said
that love will do whatever it can,
to stay alive and to be a life of its own
sometimes the need for real love is there
before its even known

for years away and away from an imperfect love
Sadiddy ran,
until that day her eyes settled *on the heart,*
and not the perfection of a man

this man
imperfect in looks
imperfect in books
had been fishing for a wife,
he had been so lonely, so very lonely
in his quiet, simple life

he was lonely for a woman
lonely for kids
he was tired, so fatigued
having searched for many years

when they met
something inside of his words moved her
the tone of his voice mis-grooved her,
his eyes lovingly cruised every part of her

Just Plain Sadiddiness

Saddidy watched his every move
as he came close to be near,
Sadiddy would find herself repositioning
he was so unsettling and creating a fear

this man,
in his presence so dense
was somehow tearing down, dismantling
Sadiddy's self-made sadiddy fence

Sadiddy had long been seeking,
but not something that would weaken,
her ability to be remain steel
how had this man gotten there, deep inside
how had he managed to make her feel?

and made her feel he did

it's a well-known fact
that in order for love to exist
someone has to give, not resist
love's ability to persist

now, deep down Sadiddy still had her ways
but that wasn't going to change in a day

now,
this man had been just as lonely
never picked up by another woman
because the truth was he was somewhat homely

Just Plain Sadiddiness

rather plain to look at,
he didn't look too good to her
no matter what angle Sadiddy sat
but he was a kind-hearted man,
who only asked one thing in return,
that she would love him
simply show him some concern

he taught her about
having kindness and respect all the while that they kissing
she had never knew she had so much to learn
this strong man made her want to listen

outspoken Sadiddy sat cross-legged
and became quiet as a mouse
he often reminded her that a real woman,
a real sister
doesn't always need to roust, things
he spoke softly but with authority
he had been sent to be her earthly king

and they fell in love, hard
and when they made love, it was hard
because Sadiddy didn't know how to share
she got angry at him when he touched her
in the wrong place
or messed her freshly done hair

but this man stayed with her

stayed patient with her
because that was the kind of man that he was
that could love a woman,
see to the heart of a woman
in spite of all that she does

he loved her outside of all her mistakes
and slowly she began to take,
all of her mirrors down
he held her hand proudly
walking her around in all the streets of that small town

because he was God sent
he loved her regardless of her past
he was a good man who never felt the need to cast,
his own judgments upon her
he knew he had to forgive her
if her humbleness was ever to occur

and in actuality,
Sadiddy died that day
and the birth of a good black woman,
a giving, kind and God-fearing woman
came to life that way

REBIRTH

I am…
a woman
beautiful and black as the night,
I can be born a second time
HE made promises to me
it's my God-given right

I can be remolded
reshaped
I can be redefined
I can make up mind
and simply choose who I want to be this time

I can cry for the first time
I can stretch myself for the first time
I can allow my worth to be weighed and handled
I can be comforted
I can be soothed
I can be nursed
I can be innocent and clean
I can be looked upon as a gift

I can be reborn

I can be forced by a higher power into a better light
I can trust that HIS arms will catch me
I can expect HIM to receive me

Just Plain Sadiddiness

I can be present in this world
and make my presence felt

and my cries for love
can be heard all over the world

Just Plain Sadiddiness

LOCAL SISTER SHEDS HER SADIDDY DISGUISE ... NEWS AT 2 A.M.

having shed her life of sadiddy conversations
and sadiddy disguises,
her days were now full of
tranquil and peaceful sunrises

full of all love and blessed prizes
a clean spirit,
chocolate babies
and lovemaking surprises

Sadiddy stepped down from her phony pedestal

she was now a new woman.
and a new life for her had begun

Just Plain Sadiddiness

GIRL, HAVE YOU SEEN THE NEW SADIDDY?

and after much loving conversation
and much loving strife
a new woman closed down her old life

no more uppity, conceited days
no more trifling ways
no more mind-stays,
of taking away,
from communities and others

Sadiddy gave in more ways
and spent her days,
becoming a good wife and mother
she took the time to speak to others

even the sisters she didn't know
the fact that she thought she hated them
was all just a myth,
because she was a black woman,
they were black women
women she had *so much* in common with

and Loneliness slowly removed her things
and went on her way to the next sadiddy woman,
of course

Just Plain Sadiddiness

who chose to be selfish and trifling
conceited and angry,
actually ugly by her own choice

CONFESSIONS OF A ONCE SADIDDY SISTER

I used to be like Sadiddy and sadiddiness kept all the love in my life at bay...

I had to stop being sadiddy so the rain in my life could stop. When I did this, when I made time for and became patient with my child; when I accepted love, in all forms, not just from a man; when I learned to love my family in spite of their imperfections; when I realized that *I* also was not perfect; when I stopped hating and plotting against my worldly sisters; when I took the time to speak to my neighbors; when I made peace with Loneliness and finally realized that she could be present in my life, but could never really take over me; when I let go of the no-good men who had no-good intentions; when I got out of bed each morning and asked God above to lead the way; when I allowed HIM to take charge of my life and show me how to reach for better things; when I chose not to drink alcohol anymore; when I chose not to smoke weed anymore; when I stopped being on the constant hunt for a blunt; when I chose a healthy body, in mind and spirit, the rain stopped. It did. Every window seal. Every gutter. Every rooftop. Every place that the rain could have landed and remained in my life, dried up. And sunshine came at me through every crook and crevice. There is now happiness in my heart. And love, real love, in all forms.

So I only ask one thing in return, that today you release your sadiddy ways.

That you, sweet sister, set your sadiddiness free!

Just Plain Sadiddiness

SISTERS, CONVERSATIONS, LIVES

sadiddy sisters
sadiddy conversations
sadiddy lives

sadiddy hairdos
sadiddy clothes
sadiddy lips
sadiddy eyes

that won't allow you to see

it's 2 a.m. sister,
pack your sadiddiness away
sleep
rest
love
be free!

Just Plain Sadiddiness

sweet, sweet sister of mine
what do you have to say,
what is all your sadiddiness
really costing you today?

Just Plain Sadiddiness

it was true,

she was born to be a writer,
just look at all the beautiful gifts
HE chose to place inside her

www.ingramcontent.com/pod-product-compliance
Lightning Source LLC
Chambersburg PA
CBHW060203050426
42446CB00013B/2966